The
POWER
& PROFIT
in Partnership

An Actionable Guide to Help Solopreneurs Grow Their Business Through Joint Ventures

Laura E. Knights & Summer Alexander

For more information or to order bulk copies, contact the authors at:
Email: info@savvysolopreneursuccess.com

Library of Congress Control Number: 2016903944

ISBN 978-0-692-66104-8

Book design by CJ Harris Creative

Printed in the United States of America.

Summer Alexander
Laura E. Knights, LCSW
The Savvy Solopreneurs
info@savvysolopreneursuccess.com
www.savvysolopreneursuccess.com

Dedication

We'd like to dedicate this workbook to all the Savvy Solopreneurs who stepped out on faith to create their own destiny.

Table of Contents

OUR STORY

Long nights. Juggling a million tasks. Endless ideas and strategies to implement. Operating as the CEO and the janitor. You may know this story. This is the story of the solopreneur in the start-up phase of their business. If you are one of the fortunate ones, you will eventually come up with systems and strategies to streamline your process before you burnout. You may even hire someone down the line, but right now, in the thick of this story, it's tough. It's hard to build a sustainable and profitable business by yourself.

We both know this story all too well. Through implementing internal systems, hiring our own business coaches, outsourcing non-critical tasks, and pulling on help from virtual assistants; we were able to grow our businesses as solopreneurs without losing our sanity. However, it was (and still is) an uphill climb. Summer was managing her marketing consultancy, and Laura was managing her small business coaching and consulting practice. And then, our paths crossed.

AN UNEXPECTED BLESSING
In 2013, while attending a small business expo in Chicago, we both listened in as the keynote speaker, Roland Martin of CNN and TV One fame, emphasized the importance of micro busi-

ness owners partnering together in order to boost their economic presence faster and more effectively.

Little did we know that a year later, what was supposed to be a one-time collaboration on a virtual business training, would actually give birth to an ongoing partnership under the banner of Savvy Solopreneur Success. Together we developed training programs, events, and other services that help solo-business owners get the systems, strategy, and support they need to move their businesses forward without losing their sanity in the process. We later expanded our partnership efforts to include both solopreneur and corporate work.

Keeping our individual businesses in tact, we made a decision to work together on all offerings where our target audience overlapped. We believe that there is power and profit in partnership and our goal is to empower small businesses to unite instead of compete, while having a little bit of fun in the process. As a result of our joint venture efforts, we grossed over $100K in our first two years of working together. We plan to continue seeking partnership opportunities that allow us to serve our clients with our complementary skill sets while also making a profit.

We were inspired to create this workbook to help you assess if partnership is right for you, and to provide you with the steps to create and maintain a successful partnership.

HOW TO USE THIS WORKBOOK

This workbook is divided into five sections that each include narratives followed by a Get It Done Action Plan. This workbook is intended for solo business owners who are looking to grow or expand their business through partnership with another business owner. The goal of this resource is to help you assess your readiness and interest in partnering, as well as provide insight on how to choose a partner and maintain a successful partnership if you decide that partnership is right for you and your business at this time.

The Get It Done Action Plans throughout this workbook include assessments, checklists, and reflection questions designed to help you apply the content to your business while it is fresh in your mind. Additionally, embedded throughout the workbook content, you will find bonus Quick Tips from our own partnership journey.

Section

2

THE CASE FOR PARTNERSHIP

SNAPSHOT OF THE SOLOPRENEUR

We love helping solopreneurs because as solopreneurs we understand the challenges they face. Let's clarify what we mean by solopreneur. A solopreneur is an individual owner of a business who is the sole employee. According to the 2018 MBO Partners State of Independence report, there are 41.8 million solo-business workers in the United States. 15.8 million of them regularly work 15 or more hours per week on their business. This number is expected to grow with an estimated forecast of 47.8 million 15+ hour independent workers by 2023. In 2018, 3.3 million of the 15.8 Full-Time Independents (people who work as independents 15 or more hours per week) earned more than $100,000, up 59% from 1.95 million in 2011 (www.mbopartners.com).

Although many people have taken the leap of faith to start their own businesses, the solopreneur faces many unique challenges. When you have to be the CEO, the employee, and the janitor; there are many competing responsibilities to navigate.

And often this "multiple personality" situation is unavoidable. We all know that much of those early start up years are experienced in the red, and don't leave much funds for the solopreneur to hire staff. Those that push past burnout and premature business closure, often find that their work schedule for their business is so unmanageable that essentially they just bought themselves another job.

The rate of burnout for solopreneurs is high, as the prize of achieving time freedom, financial abundance, and/or quitting a nine-to-five job, appears to be on the other side of working non-stop hours to get your business off the ground. We often talk about burnout in flippant terms, but burnout is real.

Burnout is a state of emotional, mental, and physical exhaustion caused by excessive and prolonged stress. When you are in a state of burnout, you often feel overwhelmed and unable to meet constant demands. Many solopreneurs who experience burnout begin to lose interest and the motivation that led them to start their business in the first place. It's definitely not a good thing, and you want to avoid burnout at all costs.

We've found that partnering together has helped us fight back against burnout, and boost productivity and profitability.

THE CASE FOR PARTNERSHIP

Quick Tip : Self-care is an important component of your business success as well. Just as you would schedule a meeting with your accountant or lawyer, it is critical to include self-care time in your calendar to help you refresh and renew as you build your business. For our year-end-review business meeting, we scheduled a weekend spa retreat at a swanky hotel to incorporate both business and self-care activities. The time away was worth every penny!

Given this, we highly encourage solopreneurs to look for opportunities with other solopreneurs to ease the weight of these challenges. We've personally experienced the benefits of partnership from our collaboration. Specifically, we've experienced three major benefits of partnering together in our company, Savvy Solopreneur Success--pooling resources, synergy, and increased productivity.

POOLING RESOURCES

One of the major challenges for solopreneurs in the start-up phase is having access to adequate capital to get their business off the ground. Depending on what type of business you have, you may need to stock up on inventory, invest in technological resources, purchase office space, hire consultants with special expertise, etc. Without outside investors or your own nest egg, it can be difficult to set your business up for success if you don't have the appropriate financial footing.

For example, let's consider the customized jewelry maker. In this (and any other) supply-heavy business model, she will make the most profit from buying her jewels, chains, and other supplies in bulk. Purchasing these supplies in small quantities, let's say for just a few orders at a time, will leave her a very small margin to pull her profit from. She may literally only make pennies on the dollar without the purchasing power to get wholesale prices on her supplies. Now, combining forces and purchasing power, with another solopreneur in the industry, may allow both of them to make more profit together than they would have made separately.

Quick Tip: When pooling resources, be sure to implement a money tracking system and profit payout structure at the onset of the partnership to track contributions and money owed to each party.

Unless you are in a business that doesn't require a lot of money to get started, pooling your resources and sharing these expenses with a partner can help you to move forward faster without draining all of your resources. For Savvy Solopreneur Success, we have pooled our resources to purchase website and graphic design resources, social media consultation, professional development training, virtual assistant services, marketing materials, event and office space, and more. We've been able to stretch our dollars, obtain much needed resources to grow our business, and keep more money in our pockets.

SYNERGY

Two minds are better than one. Synergy, or the increased effectiveness that results when two or more people or businesses work together, is a major benefit of partnership. The diversity of ideas, strategies, and perspectives that emerge from different people with different experiences and expertise can skyrocket the effectiveness and profitability of your business. We have complimenting strengths. Summer is a research whiz, Laura is a visionary, and we are both quick to move to implementation. Together, these strengths are explosive. We can go from brainstorming an idea, researching it, identifying tools to implement it, and selling it to our ideal client in a matter of a few days. That process may have taken two or three times as long to implement if we were working independently on the same idea.

INCREASED PRODUCTIVITY

For every entrepreneur, accountability is critical for success. It's easier to get lazy, overwhelmed, or just lost in your to-do list when working by yourself. When you have a partner and some-

Quick Tip: In order for your partnership to be successful, the need to compromise is inevitable. Sometimes you may have to agree to disagree or table a particular idea until a more suitable time. It will be important to know when to check your ego at the door and when to stand by your convictions at certain decision points of your partnership journey.

one to be accountable to for specific tasks that were assigned to you, there's more pressure to hit the deadline when someone else's bottom line is dependent on you. Much of it is ego. Read: "I'm not going to be the slacker of the group." Whatever the case, we've found that working together lights a fire under our butts to get our portion of the work done when we hold each other accountable.

▶ GET.IT.DONE. *Action Plan*

Before you can fully assess if partnership is right for your business, you have to have a clear grasp on your business and what you have to offer. Complete the prompts below to clarify the basic information about your business.

About Your Company

Company Name:

Contact Name:

Contact Title:

Address:

Phone:

Email:

Website:

Date business was founded:

Legal structure of company:

Licenses held:

Number of employees:

Products/Services currently being offered:

Why does this company exist?

Describe your company values:

Describe your ideal clients:

Annual company revenue:

Do you currently partner with any other organizations?

WHAT'S YOUR PARTNERSHIP STYLE?

When solopreneurs decide to partner they put themselves in a position to expand their clientele, increase their income and provide added value to their clients all while sharing the often overwhelming workload. Yet often times solopreneurs shy away from potential partnering for fear of losing their identity. Partnering does not have to be a permanent solution, in fact, there are a number of ways for solopreneurs to help each other. Three of the most common types of partnership are Joint Ventures, Strategic Partnerships, and Subcontracting.

With joint venture partnerships, each party decides to work together for a defined period of time. You may decide to host a live-event, run a virtual training program or bid on a larger corporate contract together. Joint ventures are great for partnering with another solopreneur who offers a specific and unique set of skills and expertise that you do not currently possess.

A strategic partnership is an alliance between two businesses typically over a prolonged period of time. Typically with this kind of partnership each partner is currently serving the same ideal clients in different but complementary ways. For example, if you own a catering company perhaps you would form a strategic partnership with an event planner. Benefits of this type of partnership may include vetted client referrals, providing more robust offerings to clients, access to additional target markets, and increased marketing of your business offerings.

Another partnership option is a subcontractor arrangement. With this kind of partnership, another business owner will do the work necessary to secure clients and hire you to fulfill a smaller portion the contract. Likewise, you may secure clients and subcontract work out to other solopreneurs. This is great for solopreneurs who struggle with the sales and marketing functions of their businesses but are great at what they do.

Quick Tip: If you would like to try partnering but feel hesitant about making a long-term commitment, consider a one-time short-term joint venture or strategic partnership project with a low investment. One example would be to partner together for a one-time virtual event such as a paid webinar. During this trial partnership be mindful of factors such as communication, work ethic, and customer service to gain insight on characteristics of the potential business partner.

▶ GET.IT.DONE. *Action Plan*

As you reflect on the partnership styles we've discussed here, complete the prompts below to determine which partnership style might work best for your business.

Partnership Style Inventory

What type of partnership are you looking to enter?
- ☐ Joint venture
- ☐ Strategic partnership
- ☐ Subcontractor
- ☐ Other _____

What will be the most important goal of the partnership?

_____

_____

What role do you see yourself/company playing in the partnership? (Be specific.)

_____

_____

What role do you see your potential partner playing? (Be specific.)

_____

_____

If you are considering a joint venture, what type of project may be appropriate for partnership?
- ☐ Live event
- ☐ Virtual program
- ☐ Joint contract bid
- ☐ Other _____

If you are considering a strategic partnership:

What types of businesses offer products/services that are complementary to your offerings?

_____

_____

What additional skills/knowledge could a strategic partner offer that would benefit your clients?

_____

_____

If you are considering a subcontractor arrangement:

What additional value could you offer as a subcontractor?

_____

_____

What additional value would you look for if you were hiring other solopreneurs as subcontractors for your business?

_____

_____

GETTING READY TO PARTNER

We encourage all of our solopreneur clients to look for ways to partner with other solopreneurs for all the reasons we've mentioned above. If you think you may be ready to take on a partner, here are a few points to help you do some self-assessment:

▶ **You are clear on your business model.** You know who your ideal clients are, can clearly state your offerings and the benefits and features of each one, and have a clear picture of your money including revenue, expenses, and profit.

▶ **You can directly connect partnering with increasing your profitability.** Partnering is not just about making new friends (although we hope you do!). Partnering is ultimately about helping you make more money more effectively and efficiently that you would have done on your own. If you cannot make a concrete link between partnering and increasing revenue in your business, it does not make sense to enter into a partnership.

▶ **You can share the spotlight with another talented entrepreneur.** Depending on what type of partnership you engage in, you may have to share the spotlight. In our business, we share the stage and it requires a certain level of confidence and security that allows us to not be threatened by the other's success. You will need to check your ego at the door for a partnership to be successful.

▶ **You can clearly state the expectations for what you want to get out of the partnership.** Clarifying your expectations and being able to verbally state them to your partner is a foundation for success in any relationship, including a business partnership. Clear expectations will allow you and your partner to be on the same page when creating goals for the partnership and identifying the roles of responsibilities of each person.

If you find that you could not confidently answer "YES" to all of these statements, we recommend that you do some work on your mindset and your business before pursuing partnership opportunities. It will be critical for you to get clear on these areas of your business for your partnership efforts to be enjoyable for you and profitable for your business.

Quick Tip: In addition to assessing your readiness to partner from a business perspective, you also want to take an honest look at the current state of your personal life. Are there any non-business related obligations that may prevent you from giving 100% to the partnership at this time?

FINDING A PARTNER

If you passed the self-assessment test and feel that you are ready to move forward, here are a few recommended steps for finding a partner:

1.   Review the different types of partnership we discussed above. Which one may fit your business at this time?

_____

_____

2.   Think about which partner qualities are attractive to you. This could include type of business, specific industry, type of client served, revenue range, work style, market reputation, skill sets or areas of expertise, location, etc. Be sure to consider qualities that are "on your level." You want the partnership to be mutually beneficial and not draining to any one person. Each partner should be bring something of equivalent value to the other, and both parties should be able to learn from the other. Brainstorm a list of partner qualities that are attractive to you.

_____

_____

_____

_____

_____

3.   Now that you have a list of qualities for an ideal partner, brainstorm a list of people that may meet some of the characteristics. Of course, you will have to do some more investigation here, but just create a draft list of people/businesses to explore.

_____

_____

_____

4. Once you've identified a few potential partners, send an email or schedule a brief phone conversation to share your thoughts. Once there is some mutual interest in partnering, schedule your first "business date" to discuss the potential partnership in more detail.

Use the lines below to develop some key talking points for this initial conversation.

_____

_____

_____

_____

5. At the meeting, have some dialogue together and brainstorm the possibilities for a potential partnership. Run your partner through the same assessment points you reflected on above, and utilize the Potential Partnership Questionnaire below. Explore the numbers together, as well as potential projects. It's also important to listen to yourself and consider the following: What energy are you picking up from the other person? Does the flow of the conversation feel good to you? What's your gut response to the ideas shared about a potential partnership?

In preparation for your more in-depth meeting, what are some critical points you would like to follow up on. Use the space below to write down your ideas.

_____

_____

_____

_____

_____

6. If there's mutual interest with moving forward, document your partnership with a legal agreement that details profit share agreements, roles and responsibilities, and the time frame for the agreement. We provide more information on this below.

7.   Set your timeline, revenue goals, client targets, etc. and get to work! List your next steps below.

_____

_____

_____

_____

_____

_____

_____

_____

Quick Tip : When family and business intermingle, there's a few things to consider. Developing any new project or partnership will require a time investment. Be sure to communicate the expectations on your time and financial resources with your family upfront.

▶ GET.IT.DONE. *Action Plan*

The best partnerships begin with two business owners that are thriving independently. Here is a brief assessment for you to review and reflect on your readiness for partnership. Ideally, we recommend you are able to check off all the following points before pursuing partnership.

Preparing for Partnership Checklist

- ☐ I have a solid business model.
- ☐ I have a clear understanding of my ideal clients and their unique needs.
- ☐ I understand and can communicate the difference between the benefits and features of my products and services.
- ☐ I have a clear, concise and compelling marketing message.
- ☐ My offerings are priced based on the value, outcome or transformation I provide for my clients.
- ☐ My business is currently profitable.
- ☐ I have a solid reputation with my clients, online, and in the community.
- ☐ My business is legally protected.
- ☐ Partnering makes good business sense for me right now.
- ☐ I can clearly see a direct link between partnering and increasing revenue in my business.
- ☐ I feel comfortable with sharing the spotlight with others.
- ☐ I am confident that I can communicate my expectations for what I want to get out of the partnership.
- ☐ I am comfortable with talking openly about money.
- ☐ I am comfortable with the idea of sharing profits with the right partner.
- ☐ I tend to get along well with others and I don't have a need to always be right.
- ☐ Forming a partnership will not interfere with or disrupt my current family situation.
- ☐ I am willing to sign a legal document outlining the specifics of the partnership.

As you prepare to reach out to potential partners, here are a few questions to include in your preliminary conversations. After discussing these prompts with potential partners, take some time to reflect on both of your answers to determine if a viable partnership may be a possibility.

Potential Partner Questionnaire

Date business was founded:

Legal structure of company:

Licenses held:

Number of employees:

Products/Services currently being offered:

Why does this company exist?

Describe your company values:

Describe your ideal clients:

Annual company revenue:

Do any other partnerships currently exist?

Why are you considering partnership?

What type of partnership are you looking to enter? Joint venture, strategic partnership, subcontractor, etc.

What will be the most important goal of the partnership?

What role do you see yourself/company playing in the partnership? (Be specific.)

What role do you see your potential partner playing? (Be specific.)

Describe your work style.

Do you prefer to delegate tasks or are you hands on?

Are you a planner or a doer?

_____

_____

Do you consider yourself a visionary or a detailed planner?

_____

_____

_____

Do you prefer group collaboration or independent planning?

_____

_____

_____

Your work day begins at _____ and ends at _____.

Your work week begins on _____ and ends on _____.

Is there any flexibility with your schedule?

_____

_____

How do you handle conflict?

- ☐ I am accommodating – I am likely to put my own desires aside if it will help preserve the relationship.
- ☐ I tend to avoid conflict when at all possible.
- ☐ I prefer to create win-win scenarios through collaboration.
- ☐ I tend to make quick, decisive action that may or may not include input from my partner.

Describe what an ideal partnership looks like to you:

_____

_____

_____

_____

_____

_____

MANAGING THE PARTNERSHIP

Once you've found the perfect partner for your solo business it will be important to manage the partnership effectively. In what we lovingly refer to as the "Rock Band Theory," we've found that it can be difficult to keep a partnership intact for a number of reasons. When you think about some of the most famous bands in history, you can see the destruction of a partnership filled with talented people because of personality clashes, egos, and mismanaged operations.

In order to form a successful partnership, whether for a one-time collaboration or an ongoing effort, you need to have a few key components in place. While you don't have to be clones of each other, it will be important that you have some shared values and viewpoints as it relates to business. You'll also want to have some level of trust, as there will be money involved. You will also need to create a plan for regular business operations such as regular meetings, setting pricing, marketing, maintaining financial records, client communications, and profit-sharing/reinvestment of business revenue.

And last, but certainly not least, we would be remiss if we didn't strongly encourage you to have an official legal contract in place for your partnership arrangement.

Here is your official disclaimer: We are not qualified to give you any legal or financial advice for your business, and these point are not intended to do so. Always consult your legal, tax, and financial advisors before making any major decisions for your business.

OK, now that we've got that out of the way, be sure to cover all the bases to protect yourself upfront and to be completely transparent from the onset of your partnership. Our agreement covers areas like ownership percentages for our joint initiative; how liabilities, expenses, and work responsibilities will be handled; profit share specifications; branding; terms and cancellation restrictions, dispute resolution terms, and more.

Quick Tip : Depending on the length of your partnership, it's recommended to meet on a weekly basis, or monthly at a minimum. An established regular meeting time will help you and your partner stay on the same page, hold each other accountable for roles and responsibilities, and keep the established goals and expectations at the forefront of the partnership.

Did we go into the partnership expecting to have to take each other to court? Absolutely not. But as smart business women, we understand that it's better to be safe than sorry, especially when our assets, brands, and business reputations are on the line. We encourage you to do the same. Your lawyer can assist you with creating an agreement or you can use one of the more affordable lawyer-reviewed, done-for-you services that exist.

▶ GET.IT.DONE. *Action Plan*

Managing the Partnership Worksheet

How much is each partner investing in the partnership?

Name: _____ Amount: _____ Ownership ____%

Name: _____ Amount: _____ Ownership ____%

How will you split the profits?

Partner 1: _____%
Partner 2: _____%

What percentage of the profits will be reinvested into the business?
_____%

Who will be the primary decision maker in the business?
_____
_____

What are the specific roles and time commitments for each partner?
_____
_____

How frequently will you meet for regular business meetings?
_____
_____

Which partner can make buying decisions without prior approval?

_____

_____

Who is responsible for the financial management, record keeping and reporting?

_____

_____

How do you manage products, pricing, sales and marketing?

_____

_____

What activities outside of the business should all partners avoid?

_____

_____

In the event of death, disability, disagreement, divorce or debt (bankruptcy), what will happen to your joint business endeavors?

_____

_____

CONCLUDING THOUGHTS

So, we hope we have provided a pretty compelling argument for why you should consider partnering with another solo-business owner. We've found partnership has decreased the burden of being a solopreneur while adding more success and fun to our business.

Like any type of relationship, compatibility is important but nothing is perfect without working at it. In business and in life, commitment will take you a long way. If you can see a potential benefi t on your bottom line, allow for an adjustment period to work through any challenges that may arise. If the partnership is not successful after multiple attempts, don't be afraid to cut your losses and end the partnership. Should you decide to end the partnership, maintain professionalism in your approach and honor your legal and financial obligations. And remember, just because it didn't work with one person doesn't mean it can't work with another one. Keep your eyes and ears open for other potential partners that may be a better fit for you.

GET.IT.DONE. *Action Plan*

Now that you have completed the workbook, we encourage you to use the prompts below to reflect on your next steps with pursuing a partnership. We would love to stay in touch and learn about your progress with creating a partnership. Email us your questions, comments, and success stories to info@savvysolopreneursuccess.com.

Next Steps Reflection

After completing the activities in this workbook, will you move forward with pursuing partnership opportunities for your business? Why or why not?

_____

_____

_____

_____

_____

If you assessed you are not ready for partnership now, will you consider partnership in the future? Why or why not?

_____

_____

_____

_____

_____

If you've decided to move forward with partnership...

What is most exciting about the partnership opportunity?

_____

_____

_____

_____

What challenges do you anticipate may come up for you and your partner?

_____

_____

_____

_____

What do you anticipate will be the most rewarding part of partnering with another solopreneur?

_____

_____

_____

_____

After completing this workbook, what can you commit to doing in the next seven days to move closer towards your partnership goals?

_____

_____

_____

_____

What specific action steps are you going to take?

_____

_____

_____

_____

What resources and support do you need to move forward?

_____

_____

_____

_____

What questions do you still have about pursuing partnership opportunities?

_____

_____

_____

_____

More About the Savvy Solopreneurs

Savvy Solopreneur Success is a company founded by solopreneurs for solopreneurs.

Laura Knights and Summer Alexander combined the best of their individual signature services as small business coaches to develop trainings, events and workshops designed to help solo business owners boost profits and increase client attraction, while maintaining their sanity.

In 2013, while attending a small business expo in Chicago, Laura Knights and Summer Alexander both listened in as the keynote speaker Roland Martin of CNN and TV One fame, emphasized the importance of micro business owners partnering together in order to boost their economic presence faster and more effectively.

Little did they know that a year later, what was supposed to be a one-time collaboration on a virtual business training, would actually give birth to an ongoing partnership under the banner of Savvy Solopreneur Success. Together Laura and Summer have developed training programs, events, and other services that help solo business owners get the systems, strategy, and support they need to move their businesses forward without losing their sanity in the process.

Keeping their individual businesses intact, Laura and Summer made a decision to work together on all offerings where their target audience overlapped. They believe that there is power and profit in partnership and have a goal of empowering small businesses to unite instead of compete, while having fun in the process.

Laura E. Knights, LCSW

Laura E. Knights, LCSW is an author, speaker, and executive coach that has been developing professional and personal development programs for the last 16 years in the areas of small business and leadership development. Her expertise and background in entrepreneurship, strategic planning, organizational development, and social work uniquely equip her to teach others how to deal with both the "head work" and "heart work" required to succeed in business and in life.

Laura has assisted hundreds of people through her business training workshops, mastermind groups, and popular coaching programs where she teaches people how to create a life and business of meaning and purpose that transforms their self-identity, work, and wealth.

Laura received her Bachelor's in Business Administration from Washington University in St. Louis, and her Master's in Social Work from DePaul University. She is the President of Knights Consulting LLC. Additionally, Laura is a trained therapist and holds a Licensed Clinical Social Worker designation in both Illinois and Georgia. For her work, Laura has been featured in JET, Rolling Out, WGN TV, WCIU TV, Rolling Out Magazine and several other media outlets. To learn more about Laura, visit www.lauraeknightscoaching.com.

Summer J. Alexander

With a background in market research, technology, and communications; Summer Alexander is uniquely qualified to help businesses learn to combine the customer experience with their company data to create client-centered branding, messaging, and content strategy. As CEO of Simply Marketing Solutions, she leads the marketing strategy consulting firm and has advised clients in the areas of market analysis and industry research, content development and implementation, brand messaging, community outreach and social media strategy.

Summer also conducts branding and marketing keynote presentations, staff trainings, and business workshops for governments, corporations, and non-profit organizations. In 2014 she authored the Amazon #1 bestseller The Little Book of Big Marketing Ideas. A recognized thought leader in her industry, Summer has been a featured guest expert in Black Enterprise, Jet, WGN TV, WCIU TV, Rolling Out Magazine and several other media outlets. To learn more about Summer, visit www.simplymarketingsolutions.com.

Learn more about booking The Savvy Solopreneurs to speak at your next event or conference at: http://profitinpartnership.com